a little cup of
Kindness

a little cup of
Kindness

Gentle thoughts for today's hectic world

Glenn Dromgoole

Illustrated by Kyle Dreier

BRIGHT SKY PRESS

CONTENTS

INTRODUCTION

"The world is too much with us," wrote William Wordsworth. "Late and soon, getting and spending, we lay waste our powers. Little we see in nature that is ours."

Too often, we allow the busyness and the chaos of daily living to lay waste the powers of our better selves and best intentions—to be kind, generous, helpful, reasonable and civil.

For a moment, let us sip from a little cup of kindness and reflect on what is ultimately important in our lives and in our world.

Glenn Dromgoole

A LITTLE CUP OF KINDNESS

A little cup
of kindness—
a postcard,
a phone call,
a smile
or a touch—
can amount
over time
to so much.

BOOMERANG

Kindness is like
a boomerang:
No matter
what you do,
it keeps coming
back to you.

THE BOTTOM LINE

The bottom line
isn't dollars and cents
or stock market prices
or investments.
It's how well we use
the resources we're granted,
and how many seeds
of kindness we've planted.

CELEBRATE THE GOODNESS

Look for the goodness

and brightness

along the way,

and you will find

something worth

celebrating today.

CONSPIRACY OF KINDNESS

The world needs no less

in this season

than a conspiracy

of kindness,

of generosity,

of reason.

Thankful Spirit

When we walk through life
with a thankful heart,
most of our troubles
simply depart.

With Gratitude

When life is lived
always with gratitude,
we'll find we have
a positive attitude.

Pass It On

If you've been the recipient

of a kind word or deed,

don't let it stop there —

pass it on, plant a seed.

Trilogy of Thanks

For a slower pace.

For companionship.

For grace.

Surpluses and Shortages

Too much:

animosity

selfishness

rudeness

indifference

mediocrity.

Too little:

reason

generosity

civility

compassion

excellence.

About the Author

Glenn Dromgoole is co-founder of Americans for More Civility, promoting reason, kindness and generosity. He lives in Texas and is the author of a number of books, including:

Good Night, Cowboy

Good Night, Cowgirl

Learning from Longhorns

A Small Town in Texas

Cowboys at Heart

I'd Rather Be Fishing

What Dogs Teach Us

What Cats Teach Us

What Horses Teach Us

The Power of a Penny

BRIGHT SKY PRESS
Box 416
Albany, Texas 76430

Text copyright © 2007 by Glenn Dromgoole
Illustrations copyright © 2007 by Kyle Dreier

10   9   8   7   6   5   4   3   2   1

Library of Congress Cataloging-in-Publication Data

Dromgoole, Glenn.
    A little cup of kindness : gentle thoughts for today's hectic world / Glenn Dromgoole.
       p. cm.
    ISBN-13: 978-1-931721-95-0 (jacketed hardcover : alk. paper) 1. Kindness—Miscellanea.
I. Title.

BJ1533.K5D76 2006
177.7—dc22   2006101764

Book and cover design by Isabel Lasater Hernandez
Edited by Cynthia Sellman Mendez
Printed in China through Asia Pacific Offset

Healing Touch

Kind words spoken,
kind deeds done,
time of healing
has begun.

A WORD OF ADVICE

Asked for advice

many thoughts come to mind,

but one prevails above all:

be kind.

Our Choice

We can choose

to make the world

a little better

because we're here—

or a little worse.

A Generous Spirit

A generous spirit
doesn't depend
on how much money
we have to spend.

RAISE UP A CHILD

Raise up a child to be

kind and caring,

compassionate,

generous, and sharing.

Our children will get

the most out of living

if we help them cultivate

a spirit of giving.

GLOWING

No candle can

hold a candle

to the bright glow

that fills the room

when you smile.

BETTER WORLD

A happy smile,

a friendly face

make the world

a better place.

PRIORITIES WE
WON'T REGRET

40

More kindnesses done,

more friendships sought,

more sunsets savored,

more time in thought.

CIVILITY

If we lower our voices,

respect others' choices,

we might see in the end

each other as friend.

Dignity and Respect

We are more likely to connect
when we treat each other
with dignity and respect.

More or Less

Smile more.

Complain less.

Praise more.

Criticize less.

MORE

Read more.

Write more.

Pray more.

Think more.

Listen more.

Laugh more.

TOGETHER

Work together.

Sing together.

Laugh together.

Live together.

AHA!

Most of our days,
most of our years,
most of our lives
are punctuated
with periods, commas,
colons, semi-colons,
and question marks.

But when we look back,
we cherish those
special moments
when the only
appropriate response
was, without question,
an exclamation point!

GIFTS WE TAKE FOR GRANTED

The Gift of Life.

The Gift of Time.

The Gift of Laughter.

The Gift of Talent.

The Gift of Work.

The Gift of Generosity.

The Gift of Kindness.

The Gift of Peace.

The Gift of Forgiveness.

The Gift of Hope.

The Gift of Love.

GIVE THE WORLD A SMILE

It's something

anyone can do,

an adult or a child.

We all have it

in our power

to give the world

a smile.

THREE WAYS TO SMILE

Smile first.

Smile big.

Smile often.

TODAY

We cherish

each morning,

or else,

without warning,

we perish.

LONGEVITY

You could live to be a hundred and one,

and reminisce quietly on all your years,

or occupy them with generosity and joy

and experiences and laughter and tears.

Life isn't the number of years we live,

but what we get out of them—and

what we give.

JUST FOUR WORDS

"I could be wrong."
If these four words
were taken to heart
throughout the world,
it wouldn't take long
for conflict to cease
and healing to start.

POINT OF VIEW

How could I have the
audacity to think that
I love my children
more than you love
your children—
love my country
more than you love
your country—
love my God
more than you love
your God?

HEARTBEAT

Your heart

touched mine,

and that made

all the difference

in my corner

of the world.

WE'RE JUST PEOPLE

We're just people, you and I.

We share the same space.

We breathe the same air.

We dream the same dreams.

We seek the same love.

We grasp the same hope.

We weep the same tears.

United. Divided. Why?

We're just people, you and I.

The Best Exercise

A walk in the park,

a vigorous stroll,

it's good for the heart,

and great for the soul.

ALL WE ASK

A grateful heart

A loving soul

A generous will

A humble spirit

FRIENDS AND ENEMIES

My enemy
is a friend
I haven't yet
discovered.
And I am
the friend he
hasn't yet
discovered.

WHAT MATTERS?

What unifies us
counts more than
what separates us—
or should!

A Gift of Time

Time is a gift
we do not earn,
but are free to
give in return.

Respite

Turn off the TV
and unplug the phone,
and bask in the serenity
of a quiet night alone.

THE POWER OF AN HOUR

Day by day,

hour by hour,

minute by minute,

we have the power.

THE TIME OF OUR LIVES

If we take time to

nourish our values,

we will experience

the time of our lives.

87

TIME TO WASTE

A few spare moments
with nothing to do
and no place to be
and no one talking
no music playing
nowhere to rush to
just sit and reflect
on the gentle gift
of a little time
preciously wasted.

TIME WELL SPENT

Just be there

and smile

and stay awhile

and show you care.

OUR TIME

Our time
is not our own,
it is simply
on loan,
and we pay
the interest
by taking
an interest.

THE BEAUTY WE SEE

We can find beauty —
or we cannot —
depending on what
we expect to see.

95

In the Spirit

A spiritual life,
it's been shown
throughout time,
doesn't require tomes
of a doctrinal plan.
It's simply trying
in all things
to be kind,
and doing for others
whatever we can.

A Religious Question

Do we want

to argue

our faith—

or practice it?

THE HIGH ROAD

When we reflect

on choices made

and routes taken,

we respect ourselves most

for those times

when we took

the high road,

not the shortcut.

A Prayer

May your days be filled with beauty,

your hours with joy,

your moments with peace,

and your life with grace.

A Prayer for Patience

Dear God,

Give me

more patience.

Right now!

Amen.

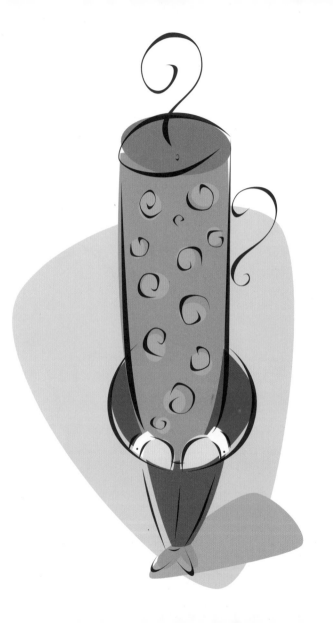

GIVEN A CHANCE

24

We're given a chance
every day that we live,
to be of some service,
to be kind and to give.

THE TRUE JOY OF GIVING

Concentrate on what you have
and not on what you don't.
Think of all that you can give
instead of all you want.
Happy people come to see
the true joy of living
doesn't stem from what we get,
but from what we're giving.

23